GRAND PRIX IMAGES

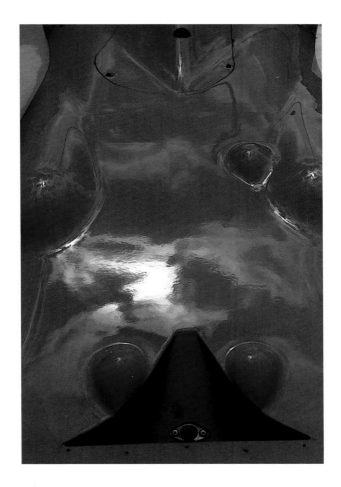

HAZLETON PUBLISHING
RICHMOND, SURREY

GRAND PRIX IMAGES

PUBLISHER
Richard Poulter

EXECUTIVE PUBLISHER
Elizabeth Le Breton

ART EDITOR
Steve Small

HOUSE EDITOR
S. G. Spark

ISBN: 0-905138-52-X

Typeset by: Solo Graphics Ltd, Twickenham, Middlesex.
Colour Reproduction by: Adroit Photo Litho Ltd, Birmingham.
Printed by: Ebenezer Baylis & Son Ltd, Worcester.
Bound by: Norton Bridge Bookbinders Ltd, Letchworth, Herts.

UK distribution by Osprey Publishing Ltd, 12-14 Long Acre, London WC2E 9LP.
North American distribution by Motorbooks International, Osceola, Wisconsin 54020, USA.

Colour Photography by:
Patrick Behar
Gérard Berthoud
Malcolm Bryan
Diana Burnett
Paul-Henri Cahier
John Colley
Lukas Gorys
International Press Agency
Kos
Dominique Leroy
Marlboro
Mark Newcombe
Graham Smith
Nigel Snowdon
Keith Sutton

Title page photograph:
Formula 1 erotica? The extraordinary image as seen by Paul-Henri Cahier is in fact the bodywork of the Benetton which covers the engine and gearbox.

Front cover photograph:
Gerhard Berger in the Ferrari at Monaco 1987.
Photo: Paul-Henri Cahier

Back cover photograph:
Double World Champion Alain Prost in the Marlboro McLaren-TAG at the 1987 French Grand Prix
Photo: Paul-Henri Cahier

CONTENTS

Captures the colour and excitement of Formula 1
motor racing with outstanding, unusual and
exciting pictures, taken by many of the sport's
leading photographers

THE RACE TO THE GRID
By Maurice Hamilton

It is estimated that more than 750 million people watch Grand Prix racing on television. What they see is the colourful tip of a multi-million dollar iceberg. Beneath the surface is a highly motivated industry, one which represents the most striking example of the collision between commercial influence and sporting endeavour. The drivers are among the top earners in sport, but perhaps that's as it should be in a game where the bottom line is losing your life.

Tragedy no longer plays a leading role now that Grand Prix racing has been made more secure by an awareness of safety and the introduction of life-saving materials and methods. But misfortune continues to stalk the race tracks of the world and it would be foolish to believe that the element of danger does not give motor sport added impetus. No-one wants to see a driver injured but the thrill of watching him balance on a thin wire, continually raised to new heights by technology, remains addictive to spectators. And to the teams and drivers.

The aim is to achieve ultimate performance without either tempting fate or stepping beyond the stringent regulations. And, with the advent of sponsorship, the need to succeed is multiplied almost in direct proportion to the amount of money invested in a team. A leading Grand Prix team running two top drivers in 1988 will ask for up to $15m.

How will the money be spent? Contrary to the popular image, Grand Prix racing is not the playground of the rich dilettante. These wealthy extroverts turn up from time to time, complete with boats, helicopters and mobile garden parties, but they are soon overwhelmed by the sheer professionalism which is necessary to succeed in one of the most expensive sports in the world. Money, by itself, is not enough. You need to know how to utilise it and the top teams are expert at that. There's no point in owning a cellar-full of Moët et Chandon if your driver never gets the opportunity to waste it at the end of the race.

Earning a salary of, in the case of proven Grand Prix winners, at least $2m per annum, they may feel entitled to spray champagne from the top level of the victory podium. It represents a release of the tension which brews during the course of the weekend and it signals the end of a job well done, not only by the driver, but also by a workforce of up to 120 people who helped to get him there. And this explains where much of the money goes.

The Williams team, for whom Nigel Mansell drives, operates out of a 53,000 sq. ft factory at Didcot in Oxfordshire. The plush McLaren factory in Surrey is even bigger and has earned the name 'The Woking Hilton'. Inside each is a team of design engineers, an aerodynamicist, a systems engineer, an expert in the composites which go into the construction of the chassis and, of course, the mechanics who build the cars.

Around 35 members of the team travel to the 16 races scattered from Rio de Janeiro in Brazil to Budapest in Hungary and Adelaide in Australia. A separate team will travel to test sessions between the races and that alone can account for $700,000 of the team's budget. This is without any reference to the cost of actually building the cars. Williams, for example, have a quarter-scale wind tunnel and an autoclave for curing the carbon-fibre chassis. Up to eight cars will be built during a season, which will leave very little change from $2m for that process alone.

It should now become clear why firms such as Marlboro, Canon, Mobil Oil and ICI are each required to inject in excess of $2m. In return, they receive exposure on television and can use Grand Prix racing as a platform on which to entertain clients and to increase public awareness of the company. Winning adds the gilt to the operation, whereas failure adds guilt to the teams if they don't succeed in front of their enthusiastic sponsors.

Grand Prix racing, therefore, is more than the 100 minutes of action seen on your television screen. With the help of the excellent photographic work on the following pages, let's step behind the scenes and take a look at the preparations leading up to the start of a typical Grand Prix.

If the circuit is in Europe, the top teams will almost certainly have made a preliminary visit to carry out tests with one car. Think of the cost of a motoring holiday abroad. Now multiply the figure by ten. That's how much it costs to ship a transporter and the crew to, say, Italy. And the race is still four weeks away!

Once at the race track, the teams operate out of vast articulated lorries which are designed to carry up to four cars. More importantly, they are fitted out to become an extension of the factory once they have been backed into the paddock and parked by the rear door of the team's pit. Apart from carrying every conceivable spare part which might be needed during a Grand Prix meeting, the truck provides facilities for modifying and, to an extent, manufacturing the various bits and pieces which might be required when practice gets under way.

Practice begins on Friday but the mechanics will arrive the previous day, unload and put the finishing touches to the cars. That done, Thursday evening is a rare night off. The serious business gets under way at the stroke of 10.00 the following morning.

These days, Grand Prix racing is a highly organised sport run on strict business lines. Everything is geared to that 10.0 start and by 9.55 a.m. the drivers will be strapped in the cockpits, waiting to begin a routine series of checks and experiments as the cars are tuned to the circuit in question. If practice does not start on time, the organisers had better have a good reason for the delay otherwise they will receive a hefty fine for their tardiness.

Each circuit is different. At Rio de Janeiro, the track is fast and flat and, unusually, runs in an anticlockwise direction. That puts the driver's neck, more accustomed to the pummelling dealt out by right-hand bends predominating elsewhere, under increased strain from the higher number of fast left-handers at Rio.

Monaco, Detroit and Adelaide are run on public roads which have, of course, been closed for the occasion. These circuits are angular and bumpy and the Grand Prix cars find difficulty in coming to terms with the trappings of everyday motoring such as white lines, manhole covers, gutters and kerbs.

A Grand Prix car – or more accurately, Formula 1 car – is more at home on the smooth asphalt of a purpose-built circuit such as Paul Ricard in France or Budapest in Hungary. Even then, conditions vary. Ricard is level and rather bland; the Hungaroring twists and turns; Silverstone in England runs around the perimeter of a wartime airfield; the Österreichring swoops through magnificent Austrian scenery. For each circuit, the drivers must adjust their cars for maximum performance since the difference between winning and losing could be as little as a few hundredths of a second over the course of say, a 3-mile lap.

Practice is spread over two days with an hour each afternoon reserved for qualifying for grid positions. Each lap completed by a driver is recorded on a computer, triggered by an impulse mechanism fitted to his car. A driver's quickest lap over the course of qualifying will determine his starting position on the grid from the fastest in 'pole position' at the front, the remainder ranged behind him in staggered rows, to the slowest driver at the back.

Practice finishes at 2.0 p.m. each day so that the mechanics have sufficient time to take the cars apart, check and rebuild them. It wasn't always so civilised. Twenty years ago, practice was run at the discretion of the organisers and it was not uncommon for a session to start as late as 5.0 p.m., leaving the mechanics no choice but to work on the cars through the night in preparation for the following day.

Times have changed, but, even so, it is not uncommon for mechanics to work until three or four in the morning if a car has been crashed during practice and needs a major rebuild or modifications.

Everything is checked. And it's checked again. The cars are rebuilt methodically and slowly. Parts which have been in use for a certain number of miles are discarded in the interests of reliability. 'If in doubt, throw it out' is the code necessary to avoid the disappointment of seeing your driver lead until three laps from the end. Sponsors, spending millions, may find it difficult to understand why a 10 pence component has cost their team the race.

The drivers, meanwhile, will have spent up to an hour in deep discussion with their engineers as they work out the correct settings for the car in race trim. There is a great difference between running a car with very little fuel on board during a 'banzai' qualifying lap and racing with 195 litres, the maximum allowed during the race. With such a heavy load, the cars will bottom on bumps on the track surface which are barely discernible to the eye.

The car is at its most efficient when run as close to the ground as possible. The teams are prepared to put up with the bottom of the chassis showering sparks from the skid pads during the early laps in order that the car will settle at the right level once much of the fuel has been burned off. We are talking here in millimetres but, in Grand Prix terms, that is the difference between a very competitive car and one which is merely average.

Efficiency is also the key when it comes to looking after sponsors and their guests during the hurly-burly of race day. Where possible, important clients will be flown in by helicopter, taken to a silver-service lunch in the hospitality area and get to meet 'their' drivers. Knowing the identity of the man smothered in all that flameproof clothing definitely helps.

The driver will have taken part in a 30-minute warm-up session on race morning, this being the final opportunity to check the car and make last-minute adjustments. Then, about two hours before the start, the countdown begins.

Each team has a motorhome in which they can hold their debriefs and eat in privacy and comfort. The drivers will lie low, nibbling specially prepared food and sipping liquid to counteract the dehydration that results from working hard in an enclosed cockpit for anything up to two hours. It may look easy as a reclining driver holds a steering wheel and pushes pedals. But the intense mental concentration required is matched by the physical pounding dealt out by the stiff suspension on the cars and G-forces produced by cornering speeds which are beyond the comprehension of the average road user.

About 45 minutes before the scheduled starting time, the drivers appear in the pits, zip up their flameproof overalls, don flameproof balaclavas and gloves and ease on brightly coloured crash helmets which offer both protection and valuable advertising space. Considering the amounts of money involved these days, the promotional aspect of the crash helmet would seem to be just as important as its safety value.

Exactly 30 minutes before the start, the pit lane opens and drivers complete a few laps before taking their places on the starting grid. The final 15 minutes leading up to the climax of the weekend, the Grand Prix start, are tense indeed. With engines silent, the drivers kill time by talking to team members. Others sit alone by the edge of the track, wishing they could get on with the job in hand. They yawn a lot and constantly ask the time. (Most drivers prefer not to wear watches or jewelry of any kind while racing. It has been known for an identity bracelet, when ripped off in an accident, to completely strip a hand of skin.)

The 15-minute delay is to allow the television camera to move slowly down the grid as the commentators, broadcasting to 34 countries, warm up in the booths overlooking the track.

Five minutes. The drivers return to their cars and are strapped in place (it is impossible for a driver to do up the belts himself in the confined space of the cockpit). The drink supply pipe is connected to his helmet, along with the radio communication jack-plug and the tube which will feed air to the driver's mouth in the event of fire.

Two minutes. The grid is cleared of all unnecessary personnel – in other words, about 98 per cent of those present on what, for the moment, is centre stage!

One minute. Engines are started, the cars complete one slow lap and reform on the grid.

Red light.

Between four and seven seconds later . . .

Green light . . .

They're off!

Paul-Henri Cahier

THE MACHINES

Preparing for battle. The Ferraris are assembled in the garage at Spa-Francorchamps in readiness for practice for the Belgian Grand Prix. The mechanic in the foreground works on the transmission while the V6 engine sits on a trolley to his left.

Nigel Snowdon

The transmission and Ford engine waiting to be mated to the back of a Benetton chassis.

The boss lends a hand: Ron Dennis, Managing Director of the McLaren team, holds the cockpit section of the bodywork from Alain Prost's car.

Nigel Snowdon

Mechanical cloakroom. The bodywork from the McLaren and Lotus cars waiting in the pit lane at Rio de Janeiro. Even in the slightest breeze these lightweight overcoats need to be secured to the stands.

Home from home. The teams work from articulated lorries,
designed not only to carry the cars to the races, but also to
provide a workshop in which the mechanics can carry out any
modifications which may be necessary during the course of the
Grand Prix weekend. A carbon-fibre disc brake and its
enormous cooling duct (left) sit in the immaculate McLaren
transporter at Monaco.

Kos/McLaren International

Lukas Gorys

PRACTICE & QUALIFYING

The start of a long and sometimes lonely road. Alain Prost, the 1985 and 1986 World Champion, leaves the pit lane at Rio de Janeiro at the start of practice for the first race of the season. The championship trail takes drivers to 15 countries, finishing eight months later in Australia.

Lukas Gorys

Ready to go. Gerhard Berger raises his hand to indicate that he is ready to have his Ferrari started. A mechanic, crouching behind the car, will oblige with a compressed-air starter. To save weight, the cars carry a flimsy on-board starter which is only used in an emergency.

Keith Sutton

All dressed up with nowhere to go. Drivers spend much of their
time during practice waiting patiently while mechanics make
adjustments to the cars. Stefan Johansson, ready for action,
cools his heels in Rio. Note the strap running from shoulder to
crash helmet, necessary in Rio to give support to neck muscles
hammered by a number of fast left-hand bends, on a circuit run
in an anti-clockwise direction. Usually, circuits run the
opposite way.

Five o'clock shadow. A racing driver's world is more than glamour and Grand Prix. Between races, he will put in many hours of testing on a lonely race track. As the evening shadows lengthen at the Rio de Janeiro autodrome, Alessandro Nannini nears the end of another day's work with his Minardi in preparation for the Brazilian Grand Prix.

Having his shoe laces tied? A mechanic up to his armpit with adjustments to the pedals of Eddie Cheever's Arrows at Imola, scene of the San Marino Grand Prix.

Keith Sutton

Nigel Snowdon

Look out! The mirrors on a Grand Prix car may be small but
they're worth checking from time to time. Nelson Piquet keeps
an eye on Nigel Mansell during the 1987 French Grand Prix.
Mansell eventually overtook his Williams team-mate to win the
race. Note the pipe running from the front of Piquet's helmet to
a drink bottle buried in the car – an essential aid during a race
lasting up to two hours in temperatures exceeding 100°F.

Diana Burnett

Thanks pal. Nigel Mansell finds time to thank Ivan Capelli for moving his March to one side and letting the Williams-Honda through as Mansell leads the 1987 Monaco Grand Prix. Grand Prix drivers are not always so generous in the use of their mirrors while being lapped – or in acknowledging their gratitude while moving through.

Nigel Snowdon

Caught speeding. The Mistral straight at the Paul Ricard circuit in France. A Ferrari team member mans a speed trap to monitor the all-important terminal speeds achieved on one of the longest straights currently in use.

Right: **Where am I? Teo Fabi checks his progress during practice. Each lap is timed by a computer, the best effort by each driver being shown on a portable screen. The starting grid is then established with the fastest driver at the front, the slowest at the rear.**

Patrick Behar

Above: **Alain Prost describes the behaviour of his McLaren with designer Gordon Murray (left) and engineer Neil Oatley. The bodywork has been removed.**

Left: **Where do we go from here? Nigel Mansell (left) and Nelson Piquet take a break during practice at Monaco. Mansell finds time for a snack while Piquet, discussing his car with Frank Dernie, the Williams aerodynamicist, seems less content.**

27

Lukas Gorys

**Searching for that extra tenth of a second. Ayrton Senna and
Gérard Ducarouge examine lap times during practice with an
engineer from Honda** *(above)*.

**Eddie Cheever, deep in thought with Ross Brawn, designer of
the American driver's Arrows** *(left)*.

**Ready to roll. The finishing touches are added to Teo Fabi's
Benetton prior to practice for the Belgian Grand Prix.**

Diana Burnett

Kos/McLaren International

ATMOSPHERE

Beautiful noise. The roof of the Monte Carlo Sporting Club is rolled back to allow guests at a sponsor's function to enjoy a spectacular firework display on the night before the Grand Prix.

Maximum relaxation. Brazil provides the driver with a rare chance to enjoy the sun. Martin and Liz Brundle recline by the pool.

Lukas Gorys

Lukas Gorys

Minimum coverage. Miss Brazilian Grand Prix is chosen during a party at the Intercontinental Hotel.

Decent exposure. Nelson Piquet gives the sponsors' patches on his overalls an airing prior to the start of practice for the first race of the season in Brazil *(overleaf)*.

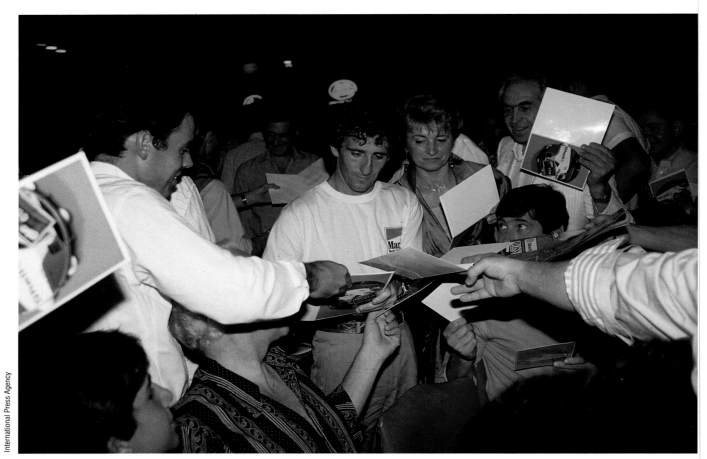

International Press Agency

Sign here. Alain Prost obliges autograph hunters.

Nigel Snowdon

See here. Ferrari fans have a clear view.

Nigel Snowdon

National divide. Serious race fans in the grandstand at Monaco while the poseurs relax in the background.

Nigel Snowdon

National front. British enthusiasts give Nigel Mansell full support at Silverstone.

Lukas Gorys

**Exclusive glimpse. Nigel Mansell's Williams-Honda negotiating
the harbour front at Monaco** *(above)*.

**Full view. Alain Prost blasts past the packed grandstands on
the back straight at Rio** *(right)*.

Kos/McLaren International

Kitted out *(left)*. Fire marshals at Monaco reflect the hazards of
motor racing.

Flaked out *(above)*. Marshals take the opportunity to relax
during a break in practice at Monaco.

Firebird. Marshals supervise the removal of a Ferrari which had come to a halt on the Monaco circuit during practice. The red-hot turbochargers are still flickering flame as the car is craned away.

Kos/McLaren International

Diana Burnett

DRIVERS

Lukas Gorys

Riccardo Patrese peers from the cockpit of his Brabham.

René Arnoux; preoccupied with his Ligier *(right)*.

Keith Sutton

**Thierry Boutsen, lashed firmly to the seat of his Benetton by
the yellow and red safety harness.**

Keith Sutton

Keith Sutton

Ayrton Senna *(left)* **and Satoru Nakajima, Lotus team-mates, show the use which can be made of advertising space on crash helmets.**

John Colley

Keith Sutton

Christian Danner *(left)* **presents a spooky image as he pulls on his crash helmet. Piercarlo Ghinzani, helmet in place, waits for the bodywork to be replaced on his Ligier.**

Keith Sutton

**Up to his eyes in protection. Michele Alboreto lost inside a
flameproof mask and the thick padding of his crash helmet.**

Kos/McLaren International

**Seeking perfection. Grand Prix drivers are seldom happy with
the performance of their cars. Alain Prost and Stefan
Johansson consider ways of improving their McLarens . . .**

Keith Sutton

Keith Sutton

. . . while **Gerhard Berger** *(left)* **and Michele Alboreto reflect
on problems with their Ferraris.**

Lukas Gorys

Nigel Mansell reaches for his neck support which helps counteract the enormous G-forces exerted on a Grand Prix driver.

Lukas Gorys

RAIN

**When it's dry, Grand Prix cars run on smooth 'slick' tyres.
Otherwise grooved tyres *(above)*, with tread patterns similar to
those used on road cars, are necessary to disperse the water
because, when it rains . . .**

Keith Sutton

. . . **it pours!**

And it pours . . .

Paul-Henri Cahier

Keith Sutton

. . . but in Grand Prix racing, the show goes on unless
conditions are deemed to be too dangerous.

Keith Sutton

THE CARS

Paul-Henri Cahier

Ayrton Senna *(left)*, **in the Lotus . . .**

. . . and Stefan Johansson (McLaren) clipping the edge of the kerb.

Paul-Henri Cahier

**Riccardo Patrese; Brabham-BMW – an Italian driver in an
English car with a German engine.**

**The vast side plates on the front wings of Nelson Piquet's
Williams (left) are designed to channel the passage of air more
efficiently.**

Keith Sutton

The French AGS of Pascal Fabre *(above)*.

The blood-red of Michele Alboreto's Ferrari *(right)* **sums up
Italian passion for motor racing.**

Keith Sutton

Arrows: British built and American financed.

Graham Smith

A mixture of sponsors for Minardi, a small Italian team.

Oriental influence. Leyton House,
industrial conglomerate from Jap
support the British March tea

Paul-Henri Cahier

Fashioning their success: Benetton's
own Grand Prix team.

Paul-Henri Cahier

Mobile classroom. Tyrrell, a team with three World Championships to their credit, have a fine reputation as the moulders of young driving talent *(above)*.

Cockpit close-up *(right)* **as Philippe Alliot hustles his Lola around Monaco.**

Dominique Leroy

René Arnoux, Ligier, uses the kerb at Monaco *(above)*.

All-German combination *(left)* **Christian Danner at work in his Zakspeed.**

Keith Sutton

**The boys from the garage next door. Osella, a happy little team
from Italy.**

John Colley

THE ACTION

The heat of competition. A turbo flames out on a Brabham-BMW.

Paul-Henri Cahier

**Moment of truth. After two days of practice, the start of the
race reveals the true story. In the most dramatic few seconds
of the weekend, the field jockeys for position in Brazil** (left)**.**

. . . and Monaco.

Dominique Leroy

The tail-enders sort themselves out at Spa *(left)* **at the start of the Belgian Grand Prix. At least there is room to manoeuvre . . .**

. . . unlike the first corner at Monaco. Satoru Nakajima's Lotus is caught in a pincer movement between Ivan Capelli's March (16) and the Lola of Philippe Alliot (30).

Motor racing enthusiasts vote with their feet at the Rio autodrome.

Patrick Behar

Paul-Henri Cahier

**The pock-marks in the track surface show the effect of
turbocharged power as the fat rear tyres search for grip under
acceleration from a corner at Monaco** *(above)*.

Right: **Line astern at Paul Ricard. Zakspeed leads Ferrari, Lotus
and Ligier.**

Lukas Gorys

Previous page: **Wide open spaces and wide-open throttle. The camera freezes the action as Nigel Mansell turns into a corner at around 185 mph at the end of the back straight at Paul Ricard.**

Malcolm Bryan

**High-speed billboard. Nelson Piquet's Williams bears
allegiance to the sponsors who invest millions in Formula 1.**

BMW
M Power

olivetti

Previous page: **Tip of the iceberg. Riccardo Patrese's head protrudes from the cockpit of his Brabham, the rest of his body cocooned in a shell which fits like a glove.**

Up the hill to victory. Ayrton Senna powers his Lotus-Honda towards Casino Square and a win in the 1987 Monaco Grand Prix *(right)*.

Nigel Mansell heads the queue. The black antenna is for radio
communication between driver and pits, Mansell pressing a
button on his steering wheel to speak to his crew.

Up, up and away! Ferraris at Rio *(right)*.

Overleaf: **Wings and wheels. The purpose of the large wings is to help keep the rear tyres in close contact with the track surface.**

Dominique Leroy

Alessandro Nannini reclines in his Minardi (*above*)**. It's not as relaxing as it looks.**

Left: **Very little elbow room in the cockpit as Martin Brundle swings his Zakspeed into a tight corner.**

'She's burning a bit of oil.' A turbo fails in dramatic fashion on Teo Fabi's Benetton.

Dwarfed by the three-tier crash barrier at Monaco, Philippe Alliot crests the rise in his Lola.

International Press Agency

Pumping out the power. A Williams-Honda on full song at
Silverstone.

Paul-Henri Cahier

**With the rev counter showing 5600 rpm, Stefan Johansson
tackles the streets of Monaco in his McLaren.**

Nigel Snowdon

Black power. Fragments of rubber torn from the tyres litter the corner leading onto the pit straight at Rio. Note the squirling marks left on the starting grid as the cars powered away.

Lukas Gorys

Respectful audience at Imola in Italy. The spectators are not waving because none of the three cars is a Ferrari!

Ferrari and Minardi: the only similarity between the two teams is that they are Italian.

Keith Sutton

It's a long march home when your car
has retired. Derek Warwick at Monaco . . .

Keith Sutton

. . . Jonathan Palmer after a hard race
with little reward in France.

Lukas Gorys

. **The flip side of the coin. Wrecked Tyrrells are loaded onto
trucks at Spa. The strength and effectiveness of the safety cell
can be clearly seen, both drivers emerging unscathed even
though the engine has been ripped clean off the back of one
car** (above).

Nigel Mansell in the stadium at Hockenheim. The white tube connected to his crash helmet supplies air in the event of a fire.

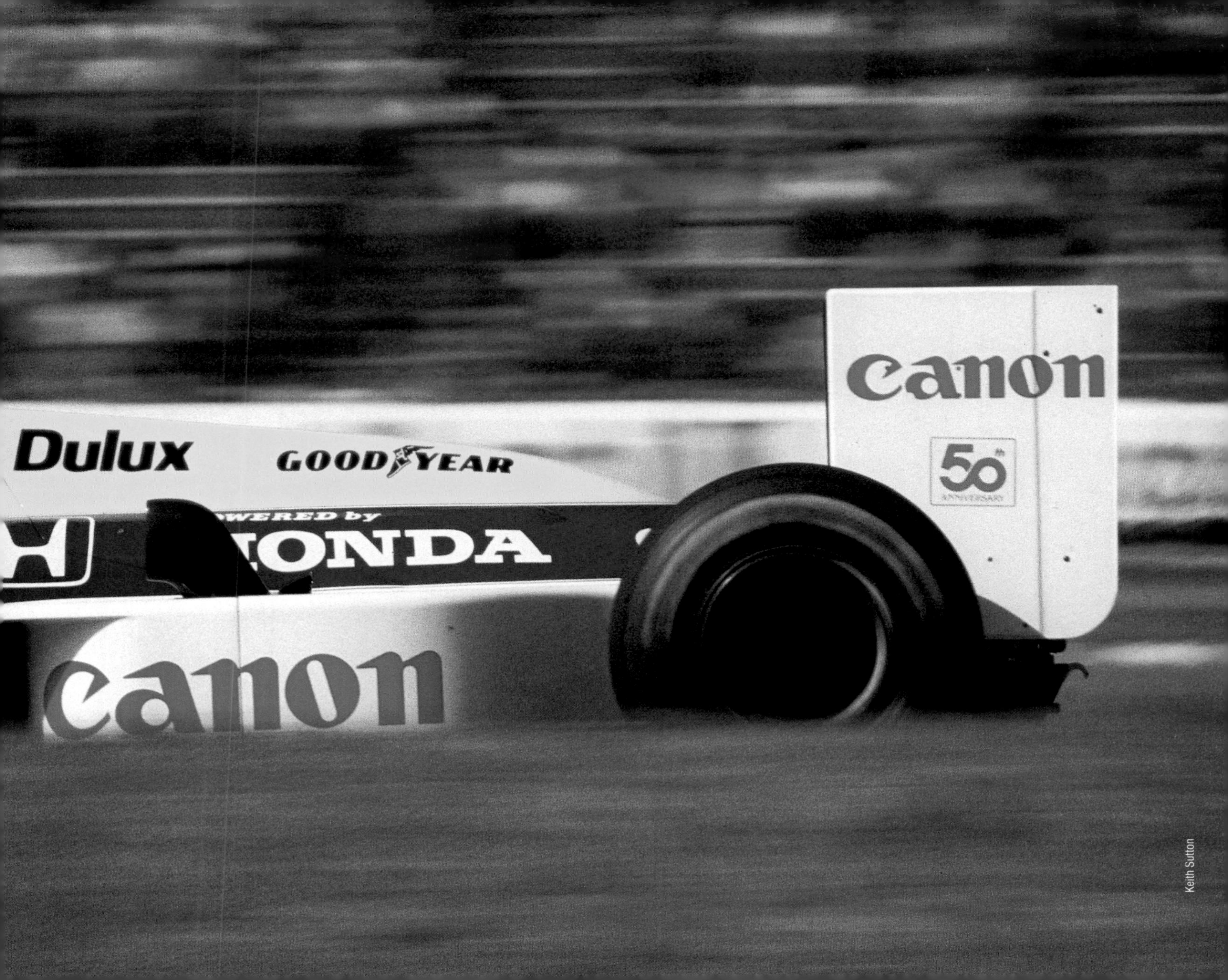

Keith Sutton

Nigel Snowdon

Above: **Exclusive backdrop. Ayrton Senna accelerates his Lotus out of Casino Square in Monte Carlo.**

Left: **Pit stops to change tyres are a strategic part of Grand Prix racing. Stefan Johansson makes a stop at Imola in Italy where the McLaren driver is further delayed while repairs are carried out to the front wing.**

Coat of many colours. Teo Fabi and the Benetton *(above)*.

Colourless contrast *(right)*. **A Tyrrell negotiates the uneven surface and a manhole cover, typical hazards encountered on the streets of Detroit.**

Paul-Henri Cahier

**Immaculate champion. Alain Prost and the beautifully
presented McLaren.**

**The Imola pit complex, with its office and hospitality suites
above fully equipped garages, is one of the best in the world**
(right).

Keith Sutton

The ribbed concrete kerb prevents Philippe Alliot *(above)* **and his fellow drivers from gaining an extra tenth of a second by using more of the track than they should.**

Right: **Yellow means danger. A marshal waves a yellow flag at Alessandro Nannini as the Minardi takes to the escape road at Silverstone to retire from the British Grand Prix.**

Alain Prost, alone on the flat expanses of Silverstone, a former
wartime airfield.

Nigel Snowdon

**Eddie Cheever keeps his Arrows clear of Monaco's steel
barriers while being pursued by Alain Prost's McLaren** (above).

An inch or two off line can spell disaster as Philippe Streiff
(left) **demonstrates by mounting the kerb at Imola.**

Paul-Henri Cahier

Michele Alboreto takes a tight line in his Ferrari.

Gérard Berthoud

**Tail section. No room for error at Paul Ricard as mid-field
runners lap a back-marker** *(above)*.

Nigel Mansell *(left)*, **every inch of his crash helmet and car
given over to sponsorship, spearheads a multi-million dollar
industry.**

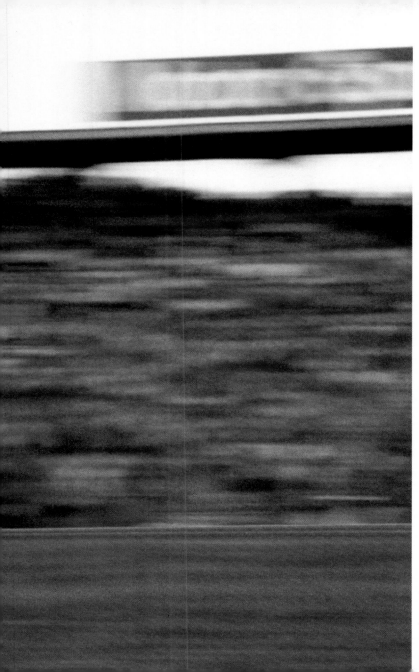

Nigel Snowdon

Emphasising the cosmopolitan nature of Formula 1, Satoru Nakajima became the first Japanese driver to score championship points. Each year more than 26 drivers from 15 countries take part in the season's 16 Grands Prix.

Gérard Berthoud

Left: **Heat haze as Alessandro Nannini's Minardi flames out.
Note the fragments of rubber thrown onto the rear bodywork.**

**Double protection. Ayrton Senna's Lotus as seen by the camera
between two rows of crash barriers** *(above).*

Nigel Snowdon

Above: **What every driver wishes to see. The chequered flag falls at Hockenheim.**

Right: **Dream moment. Nigel Mansell, his car splattered with the oil and debris of a 192-mile race, acknowledges the crowd after a brilliant drive at Silverstone in 1987.**